My Surf Tricks

written by
Roberto Diaz

Paintings by
Karen Adams

Published by **Olas - One Ocean, One Family**

My Surf Tricks

www.mysurftricks.com
(866) 238-7759

ISBN 0 9764788 5 4

Library of Congress Control Number: 2005900985

To my Muse Marla and my first-born, Garrett.

Come play with me!
Let's paddle out
and see what
surfing is all about.

I am at the top,
about to make

the drop.

I also learn
to take the

bottom turn,

and a cool

tube ride I earn.

If a wave slows down,

turns me

right around.

my cross step

is styling
and flows

to hanging my

toes

on the nose.

To pull an

off the rip,

I make sure
my feet do not slip.

A floater

is a rad ride
when over the lip
I slide.

Catching some air

can be
just like flying.
it is such a thrill
so I keep on trying.

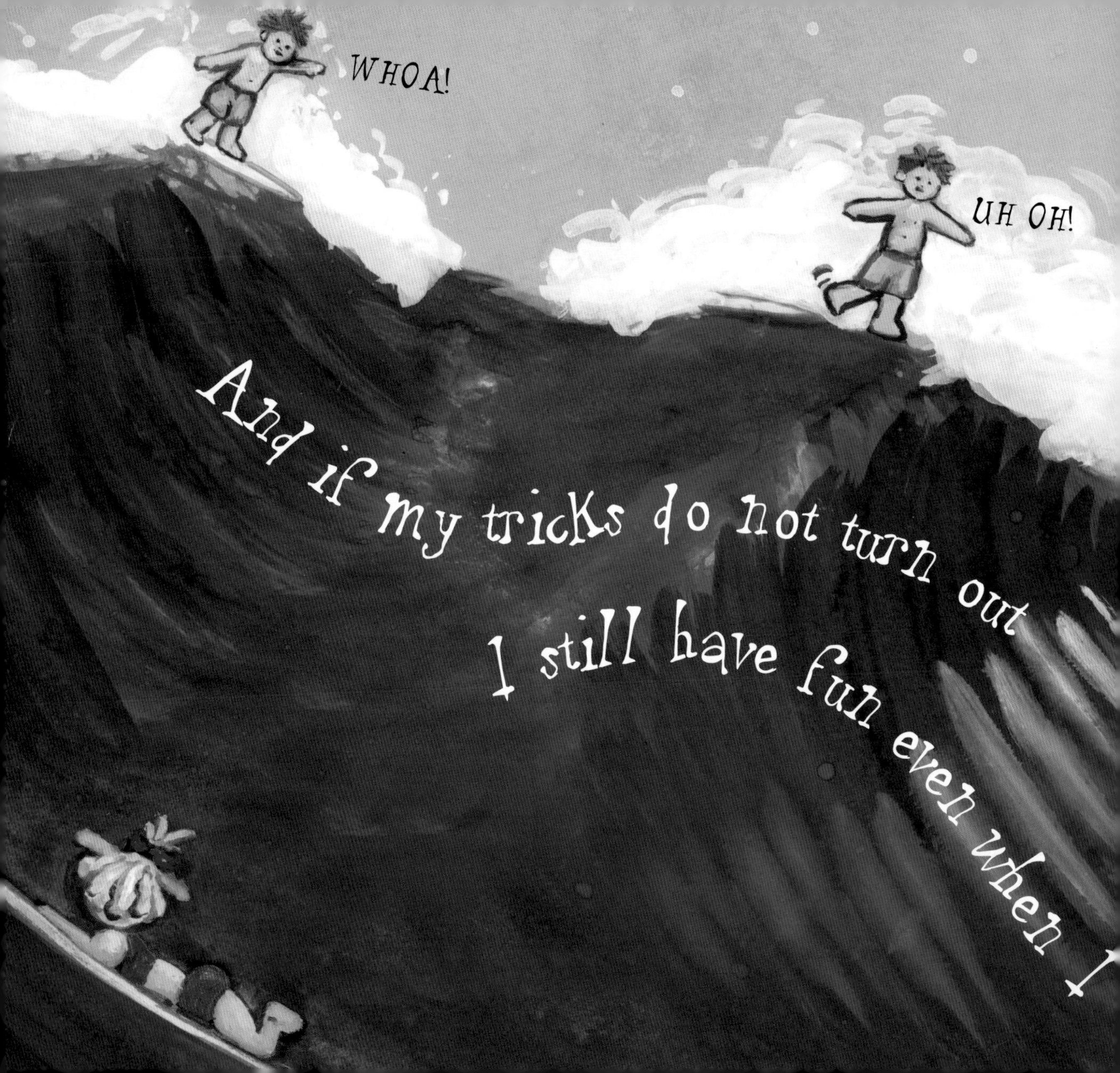

And if my tricks do not turn out I still have fun even when I

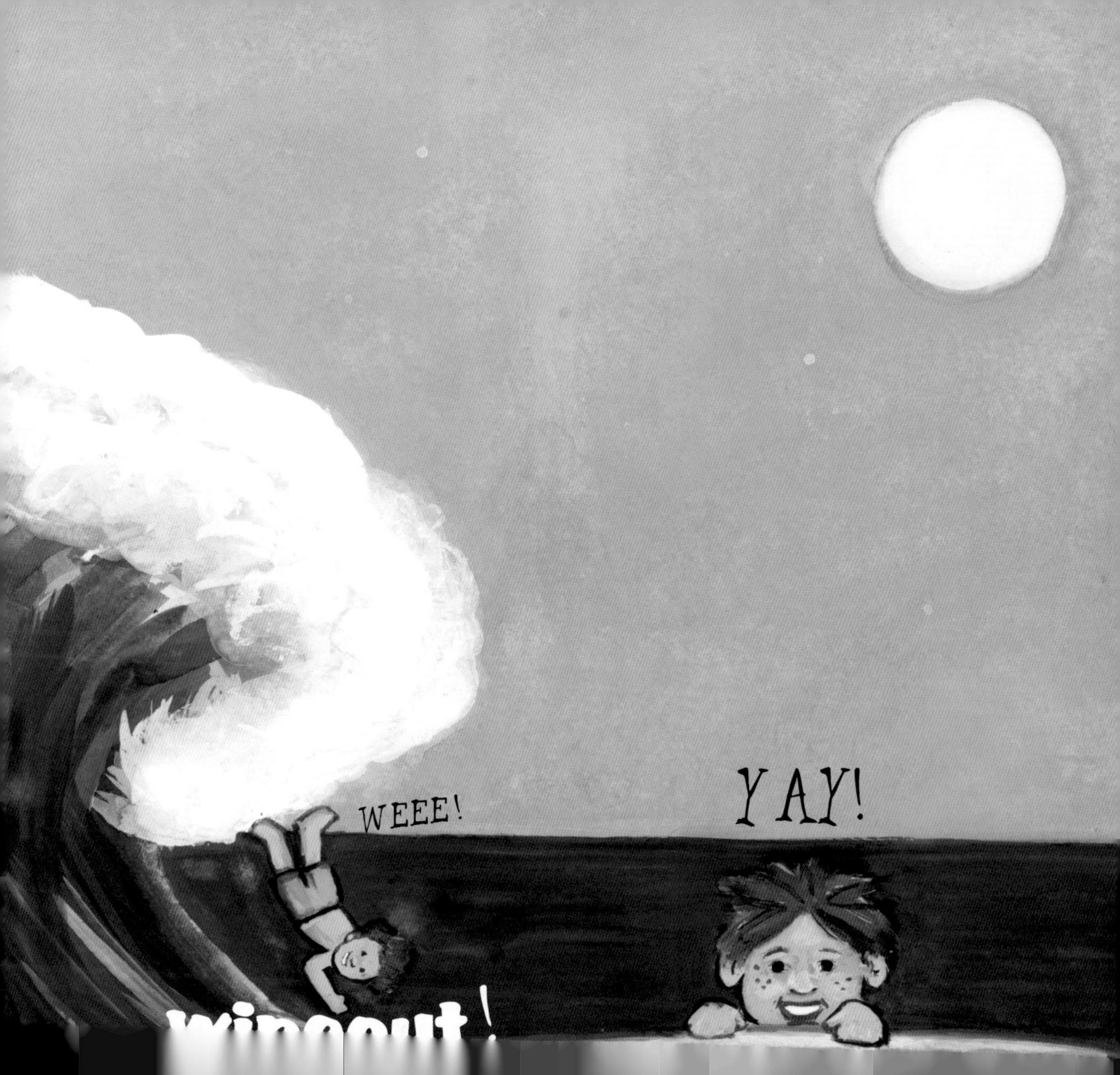
WEEE!
YAY!

The End.

Please, always help to keep our oceans
and beaches clean.

The ocean is our life!